Charles Augustus Keeler

A Light Through the Storm

Charles Augustus Keeler

A Light Through the Storm

ISBN/EAN: 9783744760058

Printed in Europe, USA, Canada, Australia, Japan

Cover: Foto ©Thomas Meinert / pixelio.de

More available books at **www.hansebooks.com**

A Light Through the Storm

CHARLES A. KEELER

And who feels discord now or sorrow?
Love is the universe to-day—
These are the slaves of dim to-morrow,
Darkening Life's labyrinthine way.
  — SHELLEY.

SAN FRANCISCO:
WILLIAM DOXEY
1894

Press of C. A. Murdock & Co.
San Francisco

DEDICATION.

You love the subtle-odored violet,
  Breathing its tender perfume in the shade,
While all the spreading leaves are dewy wet,
  In morning's jewels splendidly arrayed.
And often I have seen you low inclined,
  Seeking the timid flower 'mid its bed,
Plucking the hidden joy to deftly wind
  A wreath of love, my love to fondly wed.
So now, my dear companion on life's way,
  Loved wife, do I this wreath entwine for you:
This echo-wreath of thoughts still clogged with
     clay,
  Baffled tho' struggling towards the fair and true.

CONTENTS.

	PAGE
Life's Journey	11
Progress	12
The Runners	13
The Unreturning Hours	14
Song	15
An Arrow's Flight	16
The Stone Cutter	17
To a Floating Seed	18
Weep, Fond Heart	19
The Mountains	20
An Evening Sonata	21
To the Moon	24
The River that Flows to the Sea	25
Life's Calender	27
When the Heart is Sad and Lonely	28
Aspiration	30
A Soul's Wanderings	33
I. Solitude	33
II. The Vale of Tears	34
III. Consolation	36
Song	38
The Everlasting Promise	39
Spring Song	41

	PAGE
Youth and Age	42
Did Christ Once Walk the Earth?	43
A Fleeting Vision	44
The New Democracy	45
Stones for Bread	46
The Age Enchained. [*An Allegory*]	47
Joy and Sorrow	59
Song	60
Dreaming on the Sea	61
To a Winter Wren	62
Ballad of Annabell	63
Oh to Catch the Soul at its Start	65
A Vision of Solitude	66
Krall	71
Song	73
A Joyous Band	74
The New Teleology	79
At Sea in the Tropics	80
A Universal Prayer	81
To a Robin	84
For William Keith	87
The Return of Spring in the Mountains	89
The Voices of the Storm	90
On Science	91
A Ballad of the City	94
Death's Domain	96
Redemption	98
Ode on Sleep	100
Thoughts from the Wilderness. [*On receiving a letter from London*]	102

	PAGE
A Song of Work	108
Ode to Death	111
Niobe	113
A Spring Phantasy	116
Gently, Gently, Voices Stealing	119
Footsteps	120
Attis	122
Ode to the Past	123
Love's Rescue	124
Fate	129
To a Sea Gull	130
Sonnet on the Times	132
A Forest Longing	135
Freedom Triumphant	137
Oh Blessed Hope, Still Dream	140
The Eternal Secret	142
Farewell to the Mountains	144
To a Thrush	147
Reflections on Finding the Skeleton of a Deer in the Forest	151
Nature's Harmonies	153
Voices That Speak in Mournful Melody	156
Footprints by the Sea	157
The Unknown Region	158

Illustrated with five photogravures of paintings by William Keith, and drawings by Louise Mapes Keeler.

LIFE'S JOURNEY.

Life went a-journeying through the world,
    Where all before him was dark and strange;
In his hand was hope in its green bud furled,
    In his heart was love with its star-wide range.

Beyond him was night in its sombre wold,
    But he clasped the bud in his firm hands tight.
Pale, tear-stained Grief her sorrows told,
    And the love at his heart was moved at her plight.

On and on went Life on his endless way,
    Toward the night and the gloom of the threat'ning storm;
But the bud in his hand was green alway,
    And the love at his heart was ever warm.

And he never came to the deep night vast,
    Tho' he felt the storm burst darkly round,
For a light streamed ahead when the storm was past,
    And the green bud bloomed with the love he had found.

PROGRESS.

Slow, patient, ceaseless, striving day by day,
While silent epochs wing their constant flight
Amid eternity, each atom's might,
Crushed or exalted by the restless play
Of powers fretting at the vast delay,
Is upward pushing where it sees the light,—
Seeking expression of th' eternal right
Incarnate in some glorious array.
Call not thy seeking blind, mysterious one,
Thou pilgrim who hast scorned the formless sod,
Forever climbing nearer to the sun,
Forever reaching upward to that God,
Who, in creating thee, himself proclaimed
The loadstar of thy course—the unattained.

THE RUNNERS.

Faster, faster, faster, nerves at strain,
Heaving chests and hearts that throb with pain,
Come the runners down the track in vain,—
   For the goal is never won,
   And they stagger as they run,—
Oh the runners with the goal they never gain!

Lusty youths they are with nostrils wide,
Every one is running for his bride,
Every heart is stretched with unquenched pride,—
   As they pant with sobbing breath,
   Running towards the arms of death,
Death the goal that every heart defied.

THE UNRETURNING HOURS.

The great clock sounds,
   The time is flying,
The big heart pounds
   While the soul is dying;
The loud waves break
   On the troubled shore,
But the dead will awake
   From their sleep no more.

The red sun wheels
   From the flaming sky,
And the pale moon steals
   From the clouds on high;
So the world moves on
   From day to night,
With the dear face gone
   That has been our light.

SONG.

    It's O! and it's O!
Where the cowslips grow,
Down in the meadow my love we'll go,
Where the song-sparrow starts from his hidden
    nest,
And dew-drops hang on each grass-blade's crest;
We'll find where the breeze murmurs coolest and
    best,
There to rest, my love, to rest.

    For it's O! and it's O!
Where the soft breezes blow,
Mid the sweet-scented clover, my love, we will go;
There the warm south wind will tell us its bliss,
For never was known such a rapture as this,
And there in the meadow 'twill not come amiss,
One kiss, my love, one kiss.

AN ARROW'S FLIGHT.

An arrow's flight
With no end in sight
Through the silent night,—
Only a winging
And sudden singing
And flash of white!

Oh, arrow, arrow,
With path so narrow
And flight so far,
Not like the sparrow
That falls and dies
Is thy flight through the skies,—
Thou art aimed at a star.

THE STONE CUTTER.

Oh stalwart hewer of the stubborn stone,
  With mighty blows you shape some form divine,
Pictured in your poetic heart alone,
  Huge fashioner of life's supreme design.

Daily you hammer, hammer at your task,
  And nightly ponder while the hours stalk by;
The years roll on, you work and never ask
  To see your task completed ere you die.

Oh strange old gray-beard toiler, huge and grim,
  Forever chipping from that form ideal
The rude projections,—imperfections dim
  That cloak the lovely dreams your strokes reveal:

Oh sculptor Time, thou venerable one,
  Still hew and hammer shapes divinely dreamed,
Still work thy busy purpose, still outrun
  Thy first begettings which in childhood teemed.

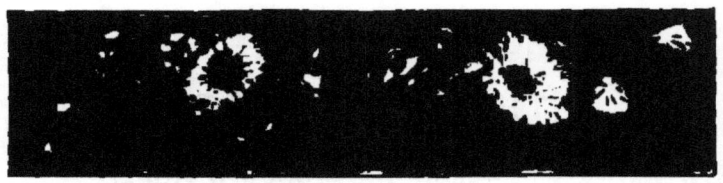

TO A FLOATING SEED.

Frail wingéd fairy, born in summer's glow,
Launching upon the world's uncertain way,
Slight, dainty voyager, brooking no delay
Upon thy course that bends at last so low;
Chasing the careless winds that round thee blow,
Or climbing at the sky in airy play
Upon thy life's one joyful holiday,
Before thou seek'st thy patient, silent woe:
Oh, seedling, when I see thee floating by,
My heart is filled with wonder and with awe
To think what loveliness thou dost imply;
What promise! what result! what constant law!
To think that thou art flowers and fruit to be,
The joy and gladness of futurity.

WEEP, FOND HEART.

Weep, fond heart, and if thy weeping
   Comfort not thy secret pain,
Trust that somewhere dimly sleeping,
   Joy will prove thy anguish vain.

Midst the bitter pangs of passion
   Lurk the hopes of joys to be,
Every throbbing pain we fashion
   Links us to eternity.

Weep, fond heart, but not despairing,
   Trust in life's intent supreme,
Love is busy still preparing
   Flowery haunts of joy serene.

THE MOUNTAINS.

The mountains! the mountains!
  There never can be
A home like the mountains
  For my love and me,
With their cool flowing rillets and pattering fountains,
  Then, ho, for the mountains!
  We'll tread them with glee.

We'll see the light deer as he leaps from his lair,
And the eagle that cleaves the far heights of the air;
We'll sleep where the pine trees are singing on high,
On a bed of their fragrant green boughs we will lie.
  For the mountains! the mountains!
    There never can be
  A home like the mountains
    For my love and me.

AN EVENING SONATA.

Divine enchantress, liquid-fingered maid,
   Trembling thy soul upon my list'ning ear,
Shaping thy wizard melodies, arrayed
   In airy garments to my fancy dear,
Let me invoke thy spell of sheer delight,
   Thy buoyant rhapsody of mellow sound;
Have pity on my music-hungry plight,
   And let my brimming heart with joyance bound,—
Beating in time with thy fast flying wings,
Threading the mazy paths of silver strings
That palpitate to feel their hopes are found
Amid the tempered joy thy pathos brings.

The lady wizard touched the keys in joy,
   While all the world seemed dancing to her theme.
What sorcery is this thou canst employ
   To waft me thus to fair enchantment's dream?

For round me fairyland is gathered near,
    Peopled with elves and fays beneath the moon,
Sporting in spritely gayety to cheer
    The sleepy flowers from their nightly swoon.
The balmy air is talking to the leaves
In mellow undertone that softly weaves
Its murmur with the idle tinkling stream,
And all the sounds that mingle in a dream.

Now comes a slow procession through the glen,
Of white-robed priests that chant a solemn song,
Of ladies with bowed heads, and silent men,
Troubled with woe at some celestial wrong;
Whereat the fairies grieve to see the throng,
And cease their merry wantonness of glee
To slip away in silent misery.
The archéd trees reverberate the strain
Chanted so deeply toward the moon-bright sky;
Piercing the dreamy birds with honeyed pain,
So sweetly sad each note did swell and die.
Then came they to a newly opened grave,

And laid therein the fairest maid of all,
And kissed her pallid brow, then sudden gave
A cry so loud and wild it did appall
The very dead that started at the call,
The resurrected dead that heard the cry,
The maiden soul that floated through the sky
With Psyche, arm in arm, while near and far
The angel form of every clustered star
Joined in the throng that swam the midnight air,
To guide the new-born maid with watchful care
Higher and higher through the dewy night,
Nearer and nearer that serene delight
That dwells beyond the confines of despair,
And beats its downy wings in ceaseless flight
Where all is love and joy and goodness fair.

TO THE MOON.

Lady that sleeps in peaceful tenderness,
   Climbing the dark pavilioned blue of night,
   Drifting upon thy destined way of light
To glad the solitude of night's distress
With silvery gleams of silent loveliness,
   Stealing through latticed clouds that breathe delight,
   Dreaming of orbéd melody, the solemn rite
Of starry conclaves steeped in blessedness;
Thou art more dear to me because I see
   Thy fair enchantments imaged in my sky,
Because my love is so allied to thee,
   My love that floats amid the blue on high;
I charge thee, lady moon, companion be
   To her I love and ever fancy nigh.

THE RIVER THAT FLOWS TO THE SEA.

Silent river, silver river, floating dreamily as sleep,
Gliding down the measured reaches toward the unrestoring deep,
Lapsing through the meadow marshes where the wild duck builds its nest,
Winding through the solemn forest, with its awful shade oppressed :

As I linger on the languid silence of thy tide serene,
Watching every rippling eddy breaking the reflections green,

Listening to the wavelets swashing idly on the
    pebbled shore,
I am filled with deeper sadness than my soul has
    known before.

As I float upon the flowing silence of the evening
    stream,
Mid the gloaming's rapt devotion and the sun's
    departing beam,
With a strange, exultant sorrow I am thrilled to see
    thy flow,
And to feel the evening stillness centered on the
    western glow.

For I hear amid the stillness rhythmic pulsings far
    away,
Telling of the troubled ocean with its sobbing of
    dismay;
Silent river, silver river, ever flowing to the sea,
Toward the sobbing, heaving ocean, you are softly
    bearing me.

LIFE'S CALENDER.

The past is dead in its grave,
The future asleep in its cave,
And the present—how swiftly flies
Its form, ere it dies.

Who says that the past is dead—
That the present lives on in its stead?
'Tis the present alone that is slain
With its moment of pain.

And the future still hovers ahead,
With its meaning undreamt, unread.
To its promise we bend our eyes,
As its visions uprise.

WHEN THE HEART IS SAD AND LONELY.

When the heart is sad and lonely,
    When the weary day drags by
Fraught with cares and woes, when only
    Sigh responds to hopeless sigh;

When we feel the incompleteness
    Mocking every thought and deed,
When we mark time's dizzy fleetness
    Sweeping on as fate decreed;

When the Heart is Sad and Lonely.

When the bursting throb of feeling
   Swelling through life's fragile day,
Striving for its woe's concealing,
   Sees the end with sick dismay :

Then, oh love, with boundless gladness,
   Heart looks into heart to see
Purple vistas through its sadness
   Stretching towards eternity.

Love looks then with eyes inspired,
   Bursting mortal chains of care,
Clasping what its soul desired
   Mid the pure unfettered air.

ASPIRATION.

My brain grows dizzy as I watch the flight,
   In free gyrations, of an eagle's drift,
In endless circles pinioning the light
   Of blue, eternal silence, 'mid the shift
Of undulating clouds. What waste too far
   For your undaunted wings to climb? What zone
Of atmospheric distance can debar
   Such vital aspirations at the throne
Of light immortal? Go, thou sluggish soul,
   Like Ganymede enclasp Jove's mighty bird,
Nor fear the giddy steeps that hem the goal
   So far beyond your ken; for hope can gird
The everlasting void that, tire on tire,
   Above us arches towards eternal rest.
Enclasp thy eagle, thrilled with glad desire,
   And dauntless seek far heaven's immortal crest.

THAT SPECTRE SOLITUDE MAINTAINS HER STATE.

A SOUL'S WANDERINGS.

I. Solitude.

With silence or the whisper of the dead,
With hollow echoes of the muffled tread
Of ghost or ghoul in mediæval tower,
Startling the crumbling pile at midnight hour,
That spectre Solitude maintains her state,
Inscrutable and vast and desolate.
I know her countenance of ashen hue
And shudder at the thought. I sadly rue
The fate that thrust me in her sombre way,
Omnipotent enchantress, with a sway
That owns no rival in her boundless fane—
Most miserable ministrant of pain.
She haunts the troubled wilderness of sea,
And shrieks to keep the fierce gale company;
I hear the wherry of her throbbing wings
Commingled with the pine that sobs and sings,
Illumined by the lightning's livid flare,

And see her folding in her arms Despair,
Poor trembling sister, shrinking at the peal
Of thunder crashing till the pine trees reel.
Thou knowest I never sought thee, Solitude,
In thy wild fits of desolation rude,
Alone with no companion save the forms
Of uncouth spirits revelling in storms;
But thou hast caught me in thy chilling chains,—
Enwoven me with darkness, and the pains
Of phrenzied sorrow, miserable one.
Oh, would thy bitter passion but outrun
Its lonely broodings, and dispel the grief
That festers at my heart without relief.

II. The Vale of Tears.

Some sound of murmurous wailing and of woe,
Of lamentations in an ebb and flow
As boundless as the ocean, fills the air,
Halting at every round of its despair.
I pause upon the rim of that dark vale,
Its damp exuberance of grief inhale,
Its darkness note, and mark each shapeless shade

That wanders restless as a cavalcade
For plunder, prowling in the dead of night.
Oh misery! I weep at their sad plight.
The cypress points its fingers to the ground,
And deep amid the gloom the howlet's sound
In ullulations quavers in my ear.
Oh bird of night, your grewsome tones I fear,
Wierd harbinger of woe. Your flight so still
I fear amid the cypress dark and chill.
Lo, as I cried, from out the blackness vast,
A huge misshapen spectre glided past—
An owl, formless, white. With phrenzied leap
I sprang upon its back, and down the steep
Went floating breathlessly as in a trance.
Now Lord preserve us from the fiends that dance
Amid that vale of tears. I could not tell
Their forms distorted by the miracle
Of sorrow deep engraved, but well I knew
How madly and how lustily they flew
About me, weeping tears of blood that showed
Vermilion drops, which through the darkness glowed

Like dripping molten beads of burning lead.
I veiled my eyes. O God, their hearts, too, bled!
And yet they died not; but I seemed to die,
Fainting and falling through the eternal sky.

III. Consolation.

Faint tones of murmuring gladness haunt my ear,
Of maiden laughter mingled with the dear
Glad liquid-throated songs of birds aglow
With love's fond passion in a world of woe;
I see the misty green of woodland trees,
The paradise of sun on dreamy leas,
The gentle flowers beaming at my side,
The stream so restful in its ceaseless glide;
And this is life that whispers to my heart
Its secret joy in tones which scarce impart
The rush of passion swelling through my frame?
The past alone my phrenzied woe may claim,
For joy and light are pulsing through the air,
And Melancholy seeks her sombre lair;
But oh, with sick forebodings I upstart,
And palpitations strain my throbbing heart.

Have I indeed escaped the vale of tears?
Like memories of hell the past appears
With all its wondrous woe.   The past! the past!
It follows me like leaves upon the blast,
But follows me in vain, for now I see
The light and beauty of eternity,
The never-ending melodies that tell
Of life, and love's surpassing miracle,
So love eternal now will shape my theme,
To murmur with its cadence mid my dream,
To sound in rapture through the checkered day,
Reaching at deeper strains of harmony.

SONG.

Now read me well
Ye demoiselle
With th' golden coronal,
   What fairy band
   In all the land
Has spun, so fine and well,
   The strands of gold
   That clasp and hold
My heart with their magic spell.

Oh demoiselle,
I noted well
Thine ear like an ocean shell;
   How large and true
   Thine eyes of blue,
And thy voice like a silver bell.
   I walked at thy side,
   Ah my blessèd bride,
My own sweet demoiselle.

THE EVERLASTING PROMISE.

In the music and the mystery that trembles in the soul,
With its endless depths of longing, with its woes beyond control,
With its fathomless abysses where the spirit loves to dwell,
With its multi-modulations that have caught me in their spell,
I have studied some forgotten, some forbidden thought or sign,
That will show the inner meaning of this citadel divine.

There is hid the joy of ages, and the sorrow of to-day,

Infant hopes are softly sleeping in the arms of chill
    Dismay;
In the weird palimpsest figured, stand the monu-
    ments of time,
Crumbling to forgotten glory in their solitude
    sublime;
Stand the promises of æons with their glories yet
    unborn,
With their triumphs and their troubles from the
    bleeding ages torn.

Deep amid the soul's seclusion, I have dallied lone
    and long,
I have heard its murmured music swelling to trium-
    phant song,
Song that permeates its being, harmonies that live
    and grow,
Winding into subtler feelings, blending into love
    and woe,
Melting into deeper strivings toward the boundless
    love we feel,
Bursting into raptured pæons of the one supreme
    ideal.

SPRING SONG.

Oh the gladsome onrushing
   Of birds in the Spring,
And the loosed waters gushing,
   When every live thing
Finds a tongue for rejoicing,
   And each silent clod
Upsprings, and is voicing
   The bounty of God.

With the butterfly's slipping
   Dull garments of sleep,
The swallow's light dipping,
   The squirrel's free leap;
See, the chestnut is budding,
   The wind-flowers throng,
While the bobolink's flooding
   The air with his song.

YOUTH AND AGE.

In youth love shimmers like the vaulted bow,
In age more like the waning moon doth show.

In fitful youth a sudden beauty gleams,
In waxing age a dimming glory streams.

Youth catches at the shadows of a ray,
Age watches the eternal in its play.

But youth outgrows its fervor year by year,
And age goes tottering onward to its bier.

The world moves onward, upward. Youth and age
Mere phantoms prove in life's eternal page.

DID CHRIST ONCE WALK THE EARTH?

Did Christ once walk the earth, and did he say
    "Love one another"?
And did those words confront you on your way,
    And did you smother
Within your darkly brooding breasts the sign?
    Oh selfish mortals!
Spurning the essence of the true divine,
    And heaven's blest portals!

Could we but write upon the zenith sky
    These words abiding,
We would not see the haggard care-worn eye,
    All faith deriding.
Come, come, my brothers, write upon your hearts
    This God-sent token,
Blaze it upon the sky, in homes, in marts,—
    The spell is broken.

A FLEETING VISION.

In the gloom of the night,
In the white-gray light
Of the moon big and round,
With no murmur of sound,
A mighty form gleamed
Where the wannish light streamed,—
A man huge and stark
As he loomed thro' the dark,
With each muscle at strain
In a tension of pain.
One knee touched the earth,
And his huge body's girth
Was ribbed with bands
Of tough fibered strands.
On his neck was a stone,
His firm lips checked a moan;
He was motionless, still;

Not a twitch, not a thrill
Showed the vigor of life—
Proved the depth of his strife.
"What is strength? What is might?"
I cried at the sight.
Then the night wrapped the form
In the mist of the storm.

THE NEW DEMOCRACY.

Hammers are pounding, and forges are hot with fire;
Voices are sounding, and swelling higher, higher;
Something is building daily throughout the land,—
Deep in the soil its broad foundations stand.

Workmen unceasing, what structure do you rear?
Toilers increasing, what labor keeps you here?
Voices replying pierce the sky above,—
"The new democracy of truth and love."

STONES FOR BREAD.

"Or what man is there of you, whom if his son ask bread, will he give him a stone?"   Matthew, vii:9.

Stones for bread, stones for bread,
    We are giving them every day,
Stones for bread and a turf for the dead
    Are the riches we give away.

It is words of stone for the bread of love,
    It is stones for the bread of life,
It is churches of stone for the God above,
    For stones in this world are rife.

But oh my heart, it is bread, not stones,
    That keeps you still beating true,
And oh my soul, it is love that atones
    For the evil things we do.

THE AGE ENCHAINED.

AN ALLEGORY.

Hist! the dawning! the light as it startles the darkness!
The ghost dance of vapors that shroud the grim starkness
Of wierd stalking spectres—the waning of visions
Enwrapped in the vestment of black which imprisons
Their lonesome assembly in conclaves nocturnal!
See morning faint struggle from regions supernal,
As it blanches the moon to a pallider gleaming,
And trembles and glows to more palpable meaning.
Hist again! 'tis the sound of the seraph-throng winging
Athwart the effulgence of morning, and flinging
Sweet scattering melodies light from their pinions—
Fair sun-gods just sprung from Apollo's dominions.

How the clammy cold spectres of night shrink and
    shiver,
And cower and slink to the brink of the river,
And sink in its pools and its slimes there to wallow
Secure from the gaze of the fair god Apollo.
With mystical music and timorous ringing
Of harmonies vibrant, now soaring, now clinging
Upon their light garments, the spirit throng surges
Where saffron ethereal with roseate merges,
'Till the fair flashing morning glints crisply the
    flowing
Free lines of their figures with radiance glowing.
Upon the top crag of a mountain, tense gazing
Amid the flushed mist of the orient blazing,
And scanning the migrants of morning appearing,
A seraph is poised, as if suddenly veering
From loftier flights he awaited the coming
Of morning's attendants with music and humming.
A seraph! how nobly he stands with lips parted,
Blue eyed, from whose luminous vision there darted
Profound understanding. It seemed that his seeing

The Age Enchained.

Could pierce to the innermost essence of being,
And nourish his fancy with mystical story
Supreme 'mid the tramp of time's vanishing glory.
Untrammelled he seemed by clay's petty confinings,
Pure soul-stuff imprisoned by gentle entwinings
Of palpable æther. But oh the unyielding
Of awful necessity, pitiless wielding
The lash and the leash for the curbing and cramping
Of mortals and angels. Now fretfully tramping
He bends his fair pinions, intent upon sailing
The radiant æther, but all unavailing
His flutterings frantic. The fair host of Helios
Was piercing the blue like the white-bodied albatross.
Oh the stinging of madness when strivings are thwarted,
And the phrenzy of sadness when hopes are aborted—
The hopeless surrender, the languid upgiving
Of profitless effort. The woe of still living
Alone and imprisoned! Forlorn and exhausted

The angel bent low on the ground chill and frosted,
With gloom-sunken features, and gazed at the
    dimming
Of heaven's attendants, his weary eyes brimming
And fair wings bedraggled. With silent lamenting
Droop-headed he pondered, his soul scarce con-
    senting
Endurance of bondage, while dimmer and dimmer
He caught the far voices, and glanced at the
    glimmer
Of flickering whiteness, so rapidly melting
Amid the blue void where the sun rays were pelting.
As motionless, chilly, and white in his station,
He stooped on the crag, like a marble creation
By Angelo struck in a moment of rapture
He seemed,—this poor soul in the woe of his
    capture.
The blue arching canopy wide stretched above him,
Around him the rocks with no creature to love him,
Below him the silence hung wide as it never
The air had discovered that echoes may sever

The stillness, and rend the vast void with the voices
That leap toward the heavens while each heart
    rejoices.
How long thus in silence he lingered, what measure
Can mark, for a heart in distress is a treasure
Too sacred to gauge by the hours that vanish,
In pitiless agony striving to banish
The soul from itself. But the torture of waiting
Fell away in a bound of the heart high elating,
And the seraph looked up to a voice. Oh, how
    tender
Yet strange the cold air the dear tones seemed to
    render :
"Why mourn thus, O seraph, alone and forsaken,
Who art thou, and why have thy fellows all shaken
Their pinions afar from this pinnacle dreary?
Art tired of fanning the blue, that so weary
You rest here alone?" What fair creature had
    spoken?
Was she witch or enchantress arrived with some
    token

Of hell's foul enchantments, or angel celestial?
He gazed in her eyes but no trace of terrestrial
Taint could discover. "And knowest thou, maiden
That comest with heaven-sent melodies laden,
Not to whom thou art speaking? Of spirit forms
  dreary,
The starry host numbers none other so weary
Of strife unavailing. World spirit undaunted,
The age of the present am I, ever vaunted
By men and immortals; the age that created
The wonders of science, whereat all elated
With wild exclamations of wonder upstarted,
And gazed at my form with a strange joy that darted
And surged through my soul with a wild rush of
  madness,
'The world is all mine!' I exclaimed in my
  gladness."
Then his hearer compassionate looked, and more
  tender
To witness his woe, for his tale did engender
Sad thoughts at beholding him writhing in sorrow.

"Cease grieving," she cried, "and have trust in
    the morrow."
"So high," he returned, "mid the skies I have
    wandered,
Such hopes high exultant in joy I have squandered,
That ill can I brook this restraint. I have captured
The lightning's fierce flames and have chained them
    enraptured
To drag me through space and through thought. I
    have crumbled
The rocks where the earthquake fierce trembled
    and rumbled,
And extracted all secrets and every strange tiding
That nature had whispered to earth when confiding.
The stars I have measured and scanned, and each
    flower
Have pulled to dissect, and have left as a dower
To ages forthcoming, the grand consummation
Of intricate knowledge of each deviation
In matter and law in the universe—tested
All powers and properties nature has vested

In tangible substance.   Elated, inspired
By vaster achievements than ever had fired
The pride of immortals, I swept at the flashes
Of sun-fire hurled from the orb as it dashes
Supreme mid the universe, fiercely impelling
Its phrenzy of light from its spirit indwelling.
When lo, in an atmosphere icy and frigid
I found myself struggling, my limbs stiff and rigid,
My soul rent with anguish, a burning desire
Aflame in my breast, in my heart a wild fire
To struggle away to the seraph-throng dancing
Upon the fair brink of the morning, nor glancing
One pitying glance in their journey elysian
Upon this cold spire, my doom and my prison."
The seraph had ended.   A silence appalling
Upon the drear mountain was sinking and falling,
Like life-blood that drips in the lull of a battle,
Or the gasps of a maniac ceasing his prattle.
Each sun-ray beat hotly and burned as it dartled,
And the icicles trembled and dripped as if startled
From slumber. O God! break the stillness, the stifle,

The choking of silence—some fly-buzz or trifle
Of bird-note to show that your voice still remembers
The love and the hope which your promise en-
    genders.
At length spoke the maiden, the seraph scarce
    breathing,
With eyes towards her brow and its halo en-
    wreathing :
"You have pondered the earth and the stars ever
    seeking
For knowledge and truth, while your fair hands are
    reeking
With carnage and slaughter, with rapine and pillage.
You have murdered the plow-man and snatched
    from his tillage
The bread he had won from the soil. Ah, you
    tremble,
Poor spirit, still listen, I dare not dissemble."
Then the maiden seemed taller, her fair figure surging
With arms lifted high, and a voice that seemed
    merging

Its tones with the tempest, the peal of the thunder,
Or the shock of the breakers that roar in their
    wonder:
"Look within you, within you, within you," 'twas
    crying,
The voice of the maiden receding and dying,
When up sprang the seraph and clutched her,
    beseeching,
'Oh, leave me not thus when my soul is just reaching
Some faint understanding." The goddess more
    vivid,
Looked down on his countenance pallid and livid ;
"Ah seraph," she answered, "come, follow my
    leading,
I'll take you within your own soul, where the bleeding
Of anguish has cramped you." Then lighter and
    lighter
The seraph's wings trembled, and tighter and tighter
He clung to her garments. In eddies mad whirling
They plunged through tumultuous tempests fierce
    curling

In serpentine writhings. The vapors of battle,
With groaning of armies, and musketries' rattle
Assailed their faint senses with sulphurous burning
Of missiles of hell and destruction—the spurning
Of life—the wild carnage, the blood and the sorrow
Of sad nations wailing the dead on the morrow.
Oh the wailing, the woe, and the wild lamentation
When science is hurled at the heart of a nation,
With cruelty, craft, and the cunning invention
Of tools of destruction,—the ceaseless retention
Of hell among men ! But the seraph is falling
Still faster through space. Hark! what voice was
    that calling ?
Starvation that stalked through the land with its
    shrieking,
The laughter of banqueters merriment seeking
In mad dissipation. Now louder and quicker
The cries clash together—the leaping flames flicker,
And the clanging of bells in tumultuous clangor
Sounds forth the wild threat of grim anarchy's anger.
"Oh spare me, fair goddess," the angel implored her.

"Dost quail thus, O seraph, while still on the border?
I'd show you foul slimes where the gentle soul
    sickens
To breathe the pollution,—where every taint
    quickens
The spirit degraded, to crime—ever sinking
In cycles contaminate; draining and drinking
The vice and the woe from the pools that surround
    them,
And cursing the state that was meant to confound
    them."
She ceased, and a darkness and silence onrushing
Now mantled them deep in its folds, like the gushing
Of chaos, eternity, fate, or oblivion,—
A famine of light, the fair hope that we live on.
When lo, from the blackness there came a faint
    playing
Of light and of melody, trembling and straying,
Uncertain and groping, then clearer and nearer.
Oh light! blessed music! no tokens are dearer
Of hope and eternity. Brighter and brighter

The rays glowed above him, and lighter and lighter
His soul leaped to meet them, for there in the
    glowing,
Stood the form of his guide with her countenance
    showing,
Bent upward to God, the ideal of all being,—
The good and the true which the earthly in seeing
Creates for itself. Oh, the light and the strumming
Of harps, for the good and the true is forthcoming.

JOY AND SORROW.

I see Joy clinging fast to Sorrow's breast,
    Pressing her lips against the dark maid's brow,
Like sisters with the self-same pain oppressed,
    Exchanging love for love and vow for vow;
    For so the fates these maidens did endow,
Each in the other's love supremely blest.

SONG.

Sing, oh sing, bright warbler of June,
Thy soul's in thy song, and the sun's in thy tune;
Sing in the morning and sing at the noon,
To thy mate on her nest,
With her eggs hotly pressed
To her quick panting breast,
Sing, oh sing, thy love to attest.

Sing, oh sing, bright maiden of mine,
With a threnody mellow of love to combine,
Sing in the morning thy music divine,
My fancies to cheer
With thy harmonies dear,
In thy silver tones clear,—
Sing, oh sing, tho' thy song cost a tear.

DREAMING ON THE SEA.

While the silver moonbeams glisten on the solemn heaving sea,
I am looking, filled with longing, o'er the waters love for thee.
As I watch the scintillations as they scatter on the tide,
With a strange unearthly meaning in the stillness of their glide,
I am sure that you are near me, and I strain my eyes afar,
Scanning through the scope of heaven every pale and trembling star.

Then I hear across the water, music wafted from the shore—
From the shore of years receding I shall travel never more.
But the music swells and lingers in the stilly midnight sky.

And it holds my soul enraptured in a dim
    lipothymy.
Then I know that you have wandered from that
    shore of long ago,
Then I know that you have followed me to share
    my joy and woe.

TO A WINTER WREN.

Merry winter waif light-hearted,
    Jaunty midget clad in brown,
Autumn leaf with life imparted,
    Spirit braving winter's frown:
From the tangled brush quick darting
    Like a flash of sunny glee,
Briskly chirping, gaily voicing
    Snatches of spring's melody—
Thou art ceaselessly imparting
Gladness with your light rejoicing.

BALLAD OF ANNABELL.

Fair Annabell was a-weeping
  In the cold still hush of night,
When all save the stars were sleeping,
  And they half hid in fright.

And bitterly wept fair Annabell,
  And hotly her cheeks were burning,
And her bosom heaved like the ocean's swell,
  With the woe of a mighty yearning.

Oh why do you weep, sweet Annabell,
  When all the world is dreaming?
And what is the shame you may not tell,
  That starts the hot tears streaming?

And why do you clasp your breast so tight,
  And sigh and think of the morrow?

And why do you start in a phrenzied fright
    From the woe of your burning sorrow?

But the morrow came with its hurrying sweep,
    And Annabell walked by the sea;
She watched the white sails far on the deep,
    And thought of their destiny.

She saw them melt in the misty blue,
    Like the joy in her own young breast;
She thought of the love which is good and true,
    And her anguish more deeply pressed.

The waves looked cool as they curled and broke
    On the rocks below her feet,
And her panting heart in a moment awoke
    To a glow of fever heat.

She paused on the brink, then she leaped in the sea,
    And the waves swept over her head,
With never a thought of the misery
    That slept in their turbulent bed.

OH TO CATCH THE SOUL AT ITS START.

Oh to catch the soul at its start,
  To follow it year by year,—
To open the walls of the heart,
  On its red rich life to peer;
To trace the flagging pace,
To gaze on the ripening face,
To watch the mind as it grows
Through its trials and woes,
Through its moments of shame and of wrong,
Like the discord that jars in the song,—
It is this that we live for and cherish,
It is thus that we strengthen and nourish
Our hearts with love's plenteous joy,—
Thus our friendship we yield and employ.

A VISION OF SOLITUDE.

The night was softly sinking
   Round the mountains dim and vast,
As I sat in silence thinking
   O'er the visions of the past,—

O'er the learning of the sages,
   With their depth of wisdom keen,
And the misery of ages
   Rotting in its grave serene.

And a legend, dimly hidden,
   Quickened in my lonely brain,
Haunting me with fears unbidden—
   With a dull unending pain.

In a forest still and dreary
   (So I learned the tale of eld),
Walked a figure, frail and weary,
   In the awful woodland spelled :

WALKED A FIGURE FRAIL AND WEARY.

A Vision of Solitude.

Walked a maiden seeking ever,
   As she glided through the wood,
Joy and hope and love which never
   Came to glad her maidenhood.

Should a mortal chance to meet her
   In her forest fastness lone,
And enraptured stay to greet her,
   She would claim him for her own;

She would lure him like the glimmer
   Of the lights in wooded fen,
Ever fading dimmer, dimmer,
   In the darkness of the glen.

While I dreamed, as night was falling,
   I recalled a maiden fair
Who had startled me with calling
   Weirdly through the woodland air.

Then a creeping dread o'ertook me,
   Thrilled me at the grewsome thought,

Suddenly my hope forsook me
    And my life with woe was fraught.

I must follow, follow, follow,
    That lone figure through the gloom,
I must wander towards the hollow
    Silence of the empty tomb.

Ah, but should I overtake her,
    Pain would from my being fly,
Should I from her trance awake her,
    She would bear me to the sky.

KRALL.

A huge unwieldy fellow
   Was Krall sprawled out on the grass,
With fat face red and mellow,
   And hair in a tumbled mass.

He lay on the sunny meadow
   With an idle empty gaze,
Till the sinking sun had shed low
   Its feeble evening rays.

For he liked the hot sun's feeling,
   And he liked the soft grass bed,
And his stupid soul was reeling
   In the bliss he coveted.

But, just as the sun was sinking,
   As he lifted his logy frame,
And his half-shut eyes were blinking
   At the golden west's bright stain,

A voice to his soul came stealing,—
   His eyes were opened wide,
And a strange unquiet feeling
   O'er his senses seemed to glide.

The voice at his ear, low speaking,
   Said only the word "Awake!"
And Krall in the dark went seeking
   For the voice that to him spake.

But he found no man in the gloaming,
   "'Twas the voice of God," he cried,
And his frightened form went roaming
   O'er the country far and wide.

Krall awoke from his hibernation—
   He awoke to a life of strain;
And the joy of a dead stagnation
   To his dawning soul seemed pain.

SONG.

High oh! where the wild plums grow,
And the cool streams flow
From the mountain snow;
Where the wild rose fair
And the maiden-hair
Their love declare;
Where a nestling's call
In the still forest hall,
Or a petal's soft fall
Breaks the silent spell
Of the dreamy dell;
There I long to dwell,—
There! there!
In the pure free air,
With no thought of care,
Is the spot for me,
So wild and free,
With the woodland liberty.

A JOYOUS BAND.

What joyous band comes dancing through the grove,
    Making the archéd trees ring out with song,
While every trellised ivy, interwove
    In airy lacework, dips its garlands long
        To fondle and delay the golden trosséd throng,
And all the birds cease warbling, one by one,
    To hear such blissful music sweet and strong,
Which can the very lark's sweet notes outrun,
Sweeping in airy rapture towards the blessed sun.

Full modestly, all clad in robes of white
    Folding about their bodies gracefully,
With joinéd hands and looks of free delight,
    They sport and revel 'neath the greenwood tree,
    Mocking the toil of honey-ladened bee,
Or sipping nectar from the cream cup's rim,
    Enraptured with extreme felicity,—
Chasing the sunbeams 'mid the shadows dim,
And filling Joy's rich-patterned chalice to the brim.

WITH JOINED HANDS AND LOOKS OF FREE DELIGHT.

Thus revelling, with nimble-footed tread,
    They meet upon their way a crystal pond
Sparkling and bubbling from its oozy bed,
    Where wavy reeds and rushes swayed and conned
    Their slender stems, each like a fairy wand
Rippling its image o'er the glassy sheet.
    Whereat the ladies each with musings fond
Stooped to survey, in frolicsome conceit,
The swan-like image swimming from their dainty
    feet.

They saw reflected Love and free delight,
    The maiden Hope all clad in splendor gay,
Fair Chastity in robes of snowy white,
    And Charity, sweet maid that shuns display;
    But one lone lady stood in stern array,
And saw upon the pool, with look of scorn,
    The haughty glance and poise of proud Dismay,
And Envy's venomed gaze that rests forlorn,
Of all its native loveliness so rudely shorn.

Ah lady with the envious glance of ire,
  The pool wherein you gaze is very clear,
The lush green reeds are tipped with golden fire,
  The sun is full of love, for God is near,
  And all your sisters' hearts with goodly cheer
Are warm and thankful for the blissful boon.
  Sing, sing, ye maidens all, with accents dear,
The plenteous glories of life's sun-dight noon,
And let dark Envy mope beneath the wan-sick moon.

THE NEW TELEOLOGY.

Nothing is meaningless, nothing is vain,
In this big world of promise—this wide sphere of pain—
Every pang that we suffer as daily we plod,
Is lifting our spirits in anguish to God.

We climb through adversity ceaselessly higher,
We mount on each lowly unworthy desire,
The beast that possessed us through ages of night
Now trembles and quails in the soul's blessed light.

Through our lowly beginnings we grasp the full plan,
As the ape chatters idly and teaches the man,

And the man gravely ponders that angels may learn,
For we climb on the states that we conquer and spurn.

AT SEA IN THE TROPICS.

Softly and gently, fair sea, is thy motion,
    Pulsing and throbbing and murmuring low,
Whispering tenderly love and devotion,
    Patient, enduring through each ebb and flow.

Fair is the light that thy still wave caresses,
    And rich is the blue that thy being reveals,
Deep is the longing thy murm'ring confesses,
    Impassioned the heart which thy calmness conceals.

A UNIVERSAL PRAYER.

Eternal Love, Eternal Joy and Life!
A world of sorrow deep in ceaseless strife,
Battling with constant care's unending pain,
Repeats in woe its agonizing plain,
And calls Thy name again,
Oh Lord on high,
But hears no answering voice come thundering
    from the sky
Its wingéd triumph or consoling love—
Words like an incense altar streaming from above,
Or like the downy flight of snow-plumed dove,
Or seraph choir humming chords that strain
Impassioned joy from bursting mortal pain.
Our earthly frettings, vain discordant toil,
Tinctured with graceless deeds of rude turmoil,
Have quite forgot the sound Thy accents make,
Whisp'ring their stern command in words that shake

The soul's most secret fane with awe inspired,
Breathing its lambent breath till joy is fired,
And leaps to join its God with gladsome hymning,
Tracing in song the hopes its joy are limning.
So David sang of old,
Striving Thy living word to hold,
But we, O Lord, are waxing overbold,
And scorn Thy word divine,
Seeking to intertwine,
In coronals of beauty's garlands fair,
The wavering strands of lust's supreme despair,
And worship this alone,
Placed apotheosized on gilded throne.
But oh the pity, thus to see
Man sink from his divinity,
Catching at empty baubles in his fall,
Lifting his futile voice to call
Upon the stilted mockery of Thy life,
Oh thou eternal God within the strife,
Thou God revealing Thy unchanging form
Dimly though certain midst life's busy storm.

A Universal Prayer.

And oh the pity! oh the pain!
To see how paltry minions seek to gain,—
By pious formal vows and servile show,
By hollow words and whining plaints of woe,
By mould-encrusted forms that breed
The factious bitterness of creed—
Thy love eternal, O Almighty One!
Sometimes despair my hope would quite outrun
Were I less sure of Thy supreme intent,
Struggling and heaving towards the firmament,
Beaming in rapture where Thy gaze is bent,
Thrilling my soul with love's sublime content.

TO A ROBIN.

How cheerily thy warbling even lay
   Comes floating blithely tuned to amorous Spring,
   When trembling passion moves in everything;
How frank thy warbling sounds at shut of day
When budding lawns slope greenly on to May,
   And early moths start forth on flutt'ring wing.
   Spring harbinger, thy constant carolling
Fills me with joy when woodland paths I stray.
Oh, robin, robin, when the autumn chill
   Comes blustering from the north o'er summer lea,
   And summer songsters press to warmer clime,
Your brave sweet call still rings from leafless hill.
   Dear bird, I love thee for thy constancy,
   And for the mellow sweetness of thy chime.

ARTICULATE THY SOUL WITH BRUSH OR PEN.
(From a painting by William Keith)

FOR WILLIAM KEITH.

Speak out, ye fervent moods of mighty men,
Articulate thy soul with brush or pen;
Awake in kindred breasts the thoughts and moods
That brood about thy awful solitudes;
Create thyself in forms that cannot die,
In shapes that scorn a transient destiny;
Reveal that inner light which God has sent,
Trembling and glowing midst thy firmament,—
Thyself a world, a universe of soul,
Clinging to God as thy completed whole,
Trembling to know thy mission, vast, sublime,
Floating upon the rushing wings of time.

O painter, from thy soul's secretest deep,—
There where the weird immortal glories keep
Their mystic shadowy forms remotely still,
Glut thy unquenching mood with thoughts that thrill
Thyself and all the wondering world beside,
Awed by the beauty so serenely wide.

Infuse thyself with goodness fair, and joy,
Supreme above the morbid world's alloy
Of discontent and trouble.   Like the swallow,
Soar mid a universal calm, and follow
Thy own light winging fancy through the air,
Secure of light and joyance brooding there.

Let no confining fancies check the flow
Of beauty falling on a world of woe,
Like rain upon a parching summer plain,
Or like some sweet, melodious, speaking strain
Of music to a maniac's soothéd ear,
Spelled from the burning frenzy of his fear.
But suffer not Content's insiduous charm
Thy constant growth's unending reach to harm.
Sure of thy mighty mission, toil and strain
Through discontent, through crushing care and
      pain,
Until the sunset glory of the Lord
Bursts round thee and the world thou hast adored.

THE RETURN OF SPRING IN THE MOUNTAINS.

When winter's grasp fast-clenched on mead and rill
   Grows feeble and uncertain; when the air
   Breathes balmily of spring's returning care,
When circling eagle moults his battered quill,
And screams amid the clouds; when wintry hill
   Is dressed in tender green; when every rare
   Frail blossom beams as if of joy aware,
And merry frogs are piping loud and shrill:
Then Nature speaks in love's bewitching strain,
   Fondling the fuzzy catkins by the stream;
Coaxing the robin to his song again,—
   The forest rings with music like a dream
Of minstrelsy in days of olden time,
And hope leaps forth at spring's melodious chime.

THE VOICES OF THE STORM.

Through the gloom and the tempest that wails on
    the sea,
  Through the bleakness and blackness of night,
Wild voices are crying and calling to me,
  As they veer in impetuous flight.

At their shouting and shrieking I shudder in dread,
  From their frenzy and fury I quail,
From the cries of the merciless wandering dead,
  With the wild swaying waters that wail.

I hear the shrill sorrow of sirens that sing
  Their fury of pitiless love,
And the deep intonations of spirits that cling
  To the shreds of the black clouds above.

They are calling me, all these mad ghosts of the
    storm,
  And I falter to see them draw near;

I glance at each shapeless unthinkable form,
   As I see its weird figure appear.

Weird wandering phantoms that wing with the gale,
   What dread should I feel from your cries?
For the terror of tempests can never assail
   The soul that its fury defies.

ON SCIENCE.

The limpid pregnant air and teeming earth,
Incessant throbbing with the ceaseless birth
Of myriad souls to mortal sentiency;
The dark unfathomed wilderness of sea,
Peopled with scaly monsters huge and grim,
Misshapen outcasts from the shallow rim
Of ocean's boundless waste; the pulsing life
In dancing sun-mote waging tiny strife—
These universal wonders shape thy theme,

Phantasmal shadows through the brain that stream,
Oh Science, heavenly oracle sublime,
Thou child of progress and the march of time.
Like some old sibyl, speaking words of lore,
Thy lips hurl daily down the sounding shore,
Of destinies' far reach, their prophet spell;
The world with strained ear hears the tale they tell;
Awed, mystified with wonder and amaze,
Upon thy revelations vast I gaze.
I see the blinded stars in phrenzy spin,
And list'ning catch their echoing heav'nly din;
I see the quivering dance of atoms hurled,
In pulse beats trembling 'midst an ordered world.
All life, all shows, all shadows, all designs,
All senseless clods, all souls with sentient minds,
Display their meaning, op'ning every cell,
And whisper secrets strange as wizard spell
By magic wrought in childhood's artless time,
The fairy scenes that fade at rugged prime
Of sturdy age. Oh Science, sweeping high,
I see you straining through the boundless sky

On Science.

Of unimagined wonders dim and far,
Spanning the universe from star to star,
Tracing the struggling life from soul to soul,
And crowning life's sublime completed whole
With love's immortal coronal to thrill
A world of joy with God's completed will.
Oh Science, ministrant of God divine,
Such mighty works of boundless worth art thine,
Such labors claim thy never-ceasing care,
Forbidding respite, scorning weak despair;
But oh, full deeply ponder o'er thy task,
And deep within thy soul the secret ask,—
The hope, the light, the joy, the eager life,
Mounting supremest through the hottest strife;
The love, the passion, worship's endless call,
What truths are these that startle and appall—
What law compelling conscience with its might
To point in silence ever toward the right?
Delve, Science, deeply 'mid thy heaven-sent soul,
And clasp eternally the sacred whole.

A BALLAD OF THE CITY.

An old man feeble and worn with care,
Lived in a cellar—cold, dingy, and bare;
On a pallet of straw he lay
All the livelong, weary day—
It was in the great city
Where people are never taught pity.

One day a child in his room appeared,
A pale-faced boy in the gutter reared,
And he pitied the half-starved man
So thin and old and wan—
In the great, grim city,
There was one who had learned to pity.

He pitied the man with a beard so white,
And he loved him and clung to the thin hands tight,
He shared his woe and earned the bread
That kept them from the dead;
Ah yes, the great city,
Held one heart that knew how to pity.

He earned their bread until work was gone,
Then he stole their bread, for work there was none,
He stole their bread, and the jail
No pity felt for his tale—
It was in the great city
Where people are never taught pity.

The old man waited through night and day,
He longed for his boy with a sick dismay,
But Death appeared in his stead,
And he lay with the pauper dead—
It was in the great city
Where people are never taught pity.

DEATH'S DOMAIN.

There is a land of wizard spell,
A dreary land where monsters dwell,
A wild, forbidding dell,
With the gloomy darkness round
Broken by no human sound,
But the wailing and the shrieking
Of a host of spirits seeking
Through the blackness of the night,
In their trailing robes of white,
Seeking light, light, light.

A loathsome form is ruler here,
And every spirit thrills with fear
When they feel him near:
Huge and black, his shapeless side,

Death's Domain.

Cyclops-like, with threatening stride
Wildly through the forest stalking,
Mumbling in his aimless talking,
With his big eyes glowing red,
Burning in his shaggy head,
Filling every heart with dread.

Lo, a burst of livid fire
Wavers like a floating spire,
Shooting ever higher;
Every shrieking ghost is dashing
Towards the burning and the flashing,
Swarming with uncanny crying,
Rustling, straining, struggling, vying
Each to touch the flaming light
With their hands, so skinny white.
Oh, the dismal sight!

A crouching witch beside the flare,
With her withered body bare,
Watches, cat-like, from her lair,
When the earth begins to groan,

And the giant seeks his own;
Then the frantic spirits scatter,
Far away their pinions clatter.
" I am Death!" the monster cried;
" Lust am I!" the witch replied;
While the giant clasped his bride.

REDEMPTION.

Heavy-hearted hopes must falter
Hourly at the smoking altar
Of despairing time, forever
Destined from ourselves to sever
All we love and dearly cherish.
Every thought we dream must perish
Ere its fellow can attend us;
Every gleam the fates can lend us
Darkens when we reach to grasp it,
Like the pall about a casket.
Hush, my love, in this despairing,

Redemption.

While we mourning robes are wearing,
Weeds of thought that cling about us,
Ghastly garbs that mock and flout us,
We forget, oh priceless treasure,
Radiant love's undying measure;
We forget that in this living
We are gladdest in the giving
Of ourselves to something higher,
Slowly mounting, tire by tire,
On the recking victims lying
Underneath—our deeds implying
Weakness or misguided vision.
Oh my love, when you emprison
My existence in your sighing,
I can even laugh at dying,
Knowing that our seeming parting
Can be nothing but the starting
Of our inner life's intention,
Bursting from its crude convention,
Leaping where anticipation
Sees love's final consummation.

ODE ON SLEEP.

Rude toil of day's distempered strife,
    Tempestuous vexings breeding care,
Ambition's fretful plainings rife,
    Hope's combat waged with fell Despair:
How like a brooding Sabbath morn
    Infused with holy calm and rest
The wild-eyed woes of day are stilled
At evening, when the silvery horn
    Gleams palely through the roseate west,
And throbbing hearts with peace are filled.

Then Somnus, dusky-wingéd boy,
    On tiptoe leaves his ebon lair.
Beholding earth's returning joy
    His poppies sweep the sighing air;
Each creature, soothed by drowsy charm
    Of gently lapsing fancies' glide,

Ode On Sleep.

Nods dreamily with blissful sighs,
While Slumber's gently folded arm
   Encircles tenderly his bride,—
Oblivion dimming drooping eyes.

Oh Sleep, most kind of all the host,
   That mantles round this mortal sphere
Conspiring blessings, thou art most
   Beloved. Thy form is ever dear:
For dost thou not convey the mind
   Beyond its dwelling cramped and dull,
Op'ning the gates of fancies realm
Where Morpheus revels unconfined,
   Where shades of wonder beautiful
The soul enraptured overwhelm?

THOUGHTS FROM THE WILDERNESS.
[On receiving a letter from London.]

Peaceful and calm amid the wilderness,
    Shadowed with snow-tipped peaks against the sky,
By limpid streamlets lulled from rude distress—
    Those restless cares that sleep, but never die—
I watch the Spring's maturing loveliness
    Come trembling round me, haply breathing sigh on sigh.

No rude distraction breaks the tranquil spell
    Where heavenly Nature smiles with beaming eye;

No shrill-voiced warning surges through the dell
　To strain the heart with sorrow's anguished sigh;
No tear-stained cheeks, no palsied hands to tell
　The listless fancy tales of cares too deep that lie.

But all is beauteous, all is glad and fair;
　From every tree a bird trills forth his song;
The lusty robin floods the morning air,
　The clanging blackbirds in melodious throng
Are all too happy, reckless grown of care,
　The amorous circling hawk screams gaily loud and long.

And flowers pave the ground with varied hue,
　The golden buttercup, the trilium pale,
The hound's-tongue's clustering stars of limpid blue,
　The dappled lily weeping in the vale;
Primroses purple all the roadways strew—
　And all so silent, lovely, delicate and frail.

Has all the world grown gentle, oh ye trees,
   Ye stately firs that dream in upper air?
Has life escaped the crushing miseries
   That left it weltering once in dark despair?
Has being climbed among the destinies
   Of souls girt round with dreams, where all is
     good and fair?

Hark! hark! be still, ye gaily singing bird,
That I may catch the echo of a word
That penetrates this mountain wilderness;
A whisper of distress,
Winging across the wild Atlantic sea.
O God, and can it be
That life means misery?
Away! away! ye anguished wail,
I will not hear thy tale,
Borne on the phrenzied gale
To trouble me.
Away! away! I say.

But thou wilt not away;
Thy voice has come to stay
Eternally !
Amid this western wild I hear the cry
Of anguished souls that weep for liberty.—
The restless cares of London's sordid din,
The murky restlessness of sin
Battling with poverty and vice and woe,
The fevered hearts that glow,
The toiler glaring from his grimy lair,
The artisan oppressed with care,
The beggar fawning for his bread,
The restless thief with stealthy tread,
The mother with her infant dead,
And hope from every bosom fled :
These are the times for anarchy
To triumph over liberty—
To leap upon the blinded age
With thirsty rage,
And glut its individual hate.
Then, when its crimson lust is satiate,

'T will see too late
The blackened waste of ruined life
Left desolate by fiendish strife.
Come, come, ye voices ringing through the age
So wild and strong,
Enkindle in my heart such potent rage,
And thrill my being with the mighty wrong
Until it bursts to meaning in a song
Burthened with woe and misery,
With pitiful uncertainty,
Invectives aimed at tyrant rule
And scorn to crown time's apish fool,
Clad in convention's mouldy dress,—
With pity for distress,
And love to comfort helplessness.
Oh, love, love, love, thy very soothing name
Fills me with hope and joy again,
Thy very thought inspires a rapture sweet,
Like tread of angel feet
Threading the mazy clouds of night
When stars shoot forth a sudden light

And seraphs wing their silent flight,—
Peopling the desert wilderness of mind,
Staggering so wearily and blind,
With spectres of a glorious pageantry,
With ardent shadows of reality,
With glimpses of a far eternity,
And God inspiring all this mighty phantasy.

A SONG OF WORK.

There is no idleness in all this moving world
That lives and flourishes.
For idleness is death,
It nourishes
Its lorn existence with the dying breath,
It hovers spectre-like round tombs and graves,
It lies in mouldy vaults and dank forgotten caves,
With rotting skulls that crumble 'neath the hand.
It skulks and falters thro' the living land,
And ever cries and cries
In its death-throe as it lies.
But work and toil is life!
There's a glory in the strife,
There's a vigor in the strain,
There's a promise in the pain
Of work, work, work!

A Song of Work.

Oh the men that never shirk
Life's appointed task,
And the women who ne'er ask
If the work will ever end,—
Oh the trees that never bend
'Neath the pressure of the storm,
Oh the lusty upright form,
Oh the ever busy brain,
Ever striving to attain
More, more, more
Of the world's unstudied lore!
Hear the anvil and the hammer
How they bandy forth their clamor,
Hear the ceaseless bells that ring,
Hear the reapers toil and sing,—
Hear the buzz and hum
Of the engines, never dumb
In the sawmill, with the shrilling
Of the lumber 'neath the plane;
It is crying out in pain
That the heartless steel is killing,

Killing every forest tree,
Large and free.
Hear the sailors making sail,
Sing their chantey in the gale,
As they pull, pull, pull,
Till the flapping sail is full.
See the clerk forever writing.
See the business man inditing
Letters that will make his fortune,
While his creditors importune.
All are busy—some with good and some with evil,—
Shrewd connivings of the devil
Busy some with midnight revel,—
Such is life—all incomplete and growing,
Working, heaving, thrusting, throwing—
Working out God's destined plan,
Working for the betterment of man,
Working through the æons fierce and strong,
Bursting forth in gladness and in song.

ODE TO DEATH.

Inexorable goddess clad in night,
   Wan harbinger of woe and dismal fear,
Thou to whose dusky pinions no delight
   Can conjure respite from compulsions drear;
How often to the feast, or lightsome glee
   Of moments over fraught with passion's spell,
   You stalk with ghastly stride and stand and gaze,
So grim and pale, on one face fixedly,
   While every trembling guest, the meaning well
   Interprets as he starts in dread amaze.

I fear thy sullen footfalls through the gloom,
   The lamentations thronging in thy train,
The mournful journey to th' expectant tomb,
   The dreary progress back to life again:

A Light Through the Storm.

Thy sway is never ceasing in its spell;
   Thy incompleted mission day by day,
   Augmented by the teeming life that springs
From nature's boundless store, an endless knell
   Is sounding from the earth in sad dismay,
   While red eyes weep to feel the pain it brings.

No, Death, not fear of thy dark frown impels
   My grief at thought of thee and of thy train,—
Fantastic nightmare of the brain that tells
   Of life's defeat and sorrow's endless strain;
But thou canst part the clinging ties of love
   For some short space of the eternal round,
   And in this earthly circle leave to weep
Fond hearts impatient of delays that prove
   Too tedious. For this I fear the sound
   Of thy dark pinions through the midnight deep.

NIOBE.

When enrobed in vestal whiteness,
Glinting fair in crystal brightness,—
Frozen witchery compelling
Uncouth shapes to beauty, spelling
Life to an enraptured sleeping,
I behold thee, Winter, weeping—
Weeping in thy silent sadness;
Almost pacified to gladness
By the beauty of thy anguish,
I perforce must faint and languish
In thy presence, at perceiving
How life's throbbing pulse is breathing
In thy marble arms, like dying
Sobs of wind through fancy sighing.

Then I see, sad-hearted mother,
How thy heart-throbs thou must smother

In a sigh of music, frozen
'Midst the realms which thou hast chosen
As thy home,—to weep forever
For the children who will never
More return to still the sorrow
Which returns on every morrow.
Fierce Latona, with Apollo
And Diana swift to follow,
What stern fury nerved such slaughter?
Gentler measures might have taught her—
Poor, proud Niobe—the beauty
Of humility and duty.

But, methinks, amidst her wailing
There is still some hope prevailing,
For her children are eternal,—
Changed, exulted by supernal
Ecstacy of love undying,
Trusting through despondent sighing.
When spring's tenderness is telling
Nature of her soul indwelling,

Niobe.

When each icy spire and spindle
Softly melting, seems to dwindle
Into nothing, 'tis the waking
Of her frozen children, shaking
Winter's magic to the brightness
Of new life, the warmth and lightness
Of a loosened soul.   Revealing
Thy true self, I see thee stealing
God Apollo, armed with glances
Gay with life and joy that dances
To the brook's melodious measure.
Haste, fair Niobe, and clasp thy treasure.

A SPRING PHANTASY.

Ah, dearest, the unrestful moan
Of winter's constant wail,
In chilly fretful monotone
Amidst the forest vale,
    Has ceased its dismal chiding,
    And airy thought is riding
    Like swallow high 'mid spring's delight
    Of azure air, in blissful gliding
    Through sunbeams newly dight.

So let us linger where the joy
Most fondly sings and broods,

A Spring Phantasy.

Casting the winter's dull annoy—
The chill unquiet moods—
    Like dappled serpent shaking
    His dingy slough on waking,
    We'll wander clad in orient hues,
    In radiant robes of pleasure's making,
    Which fancy light indues.

The humming bird-shall be our guest,
Light trembling o'er the bell
Of manzanita blooms in quest
Of teeming honeyed cell.
    We'll breathe the inspiration
    Of Flora's fair ovation,—
    Of fields embossed with flowery gems;
    And worship mute with adoration
    The meadow's diadems.

With nodding pepper-grass we'll weep
Upon the woody hill,
On tender shepherd's-purse we'll sleep,
And wake to feel the thrill

Of nature's sudden splendor;
Our souls with passion tender
Enwoven deep in rapture's sky
Where saffron dawn-clouds light, engender
A hope which cannot die.

Come, love, the quail is calling loud,
The clattering blackbirds sing,
The lizard 'scapes his chilly shroud,
And every sentient thing
Is teeming with its measure
Of sweet expressive pleasure:
Come, love, we'll join the gladsome train,
For heaven is full of golden treasure,
And joy has banished pain.

GENTLY, GENTLY, VOICES STEALING.

Gently, gently, voices stealing
    From the misty gloom of years,
Whisper words of tender feeling
    Soothingly into my ears.

When by midnight silence saddened,
    I have heard those tender sounds,
How my troubled thoughts have gladdened,
    Soothed from pains unhealing wounds.

Ah, my blessed love, forever
    We are living in the past,
And the strife of hot endeavor
    Burns into a dream at last;

Burns into a dream of sorrow,
    Dwindles to a sigh of pain,
But the hope will mount to-morrow,
    And the lesson still remain.

FOOTSTEPS.

The tread of feet
Through the busy street—
How they echo and sound
On the cold stone ground.
The man with a pace
As grave as his face,
Weighty and slow
From years of woe,—
The idler that shuffles
The school boy that scuffles
And shambles along
With a catch of a song
On his puckered lips,
The maiden that trips
Light-hearted and gay
On her thoughtless way.
And the tramp of feet

Footsteps.

As the drums loud beat,
And the blue coats start
For the war's grim heart;
Or the slow, slow tread
That attends the dead
To its resting place.
Thus life's hot race
Must ever end;
Towards the grave we trend,
Yet the tread of feet
Through the busy street
Still wakens the sound
Of its endless round,—
New steps will tread
In the paths of the dead.

ATTIS.

Fair Attis stood beside the sounding sea
And looked across the waters ceaselessly,
Like some mad prophet who had caught afar
A glimpse of Phœbus in his radiant car.
Far, far away he gazed amid the blue,
While tender fancy shaped the cherished view
Which filled his gentle eyes with tears of pain
At thought of bliss which ne'er might be again.
The fair sun glinted on his visage white,
The breeze toyed am'rous with his hair, and light
The siren sea came billowing up the strand
With freight of kelp to fringe the ribbéd sand.
Oh look not thus so wildly and so still,
Poor pitiful immortal.   Hear the shrill
Of yon wild wheeling sea-mew circling high,
With storm cry threat'ning at the azure sky;
Divert your heart with anything more near

Than that far distant gaze wherewith you peer
And pierce the past, and 'neath its heavy shell
Feast on the sweet remembered miracle
Of happiness now gone—forever flown—
Shriveled within the compass of a moan,
A single storm wail or the maniac shriek
At thought of that fair past you ever seek.

ODE TO THE PAST.

Who would recall the past, or let to-day
   Too fondly linger when its hour is gone?
Who would rejoice, on life's unending way,
   To know the moment's joy would linger on?
Loved past! without thy treasured fancies near,
Without the subtle charm thy thoughts inspire,
   The wealth of rapture gathered from thy shows,
The burning madness fanned by long desire,
I know no dream in life, no fancy dear
   To lure my spirit from eternal woes.

What shows there are within thy storied fane,
  What half-remembered passions dimly sleep,
What shadows ever seeking to regain
  Their shifting glories melting as they weep;
I hear the sound of birds' melodious choir
As springs come thronging to my fancies' spell,
  I pluck again the flowers beside the rill,
And summer's whisper steals across the dell,
Infusing in my heart the ardent fire
  Of passions which the years can never still.

LOVE'S RESCUE.

Fair star that dartles o'er the crimson west,
  List to my lay,
Thou silent wanderer ever seeking rest
  Upon the brink of day,
    Thou wingéd soul embodied in a ray.

I asked thy sister of the silent morn,
    Fainting with night,
Why all things lovely linger till forlorn
    They vanish from our sight,
        Changed from their burning radiance of delight.

But she grew dimmer, dimmer, in the sky—
    The morning burst—
With never echo of a faint reply.
    I waited till I cursed
        The star and all the hopes my fancy nursed.

I cursed the star, dear orb, I cursed the beam
    That scorned my thought,
And ever since a maddened throng I've seen
    Of pallid spectres fraught
        With dim confusion—seeking what I sought.

They shrieked upon the shuddering midnight air,
    That spectre crew—

Grim skeletons in sheets—and smote the fair
    Perpetual star-meshed blue,
    Reverberating with their wild halloo.

Ah, gentle star of evening, hear my lay.
    No more I see
Those ghosts of horror, for across my way
    An angel chanced to flee,
    Wearing the emblem of eternity.

I called in agony the passer-by—
    Hope was her name—
She heard me; in her arms she stilled my cry.
    But now she is no more the same,—
    'Twas love that to my lonely asking came.

FATE.

Faint hope that breathes like fitful sighs
   Of summer zephyrs mild,
Sweet melody that swells and dies
   Amid the forest wild;
The treasured dream of promise fled,
The anguished pang of passion dead,
The grave all cold in which it lies,
   The heart unreconciled:

Ah Fate, is such your tyrant glee
   To crush the riven heart,
And do you feed on misery,
   On sorrow's burning smart?
Still restless on thy passion swells,
And care-bowed age the story tells

Of sorrow's wide supremacy
    And joy's swift fading part.

But, Fate, what realm was ever chained
    To your cold heartless spell?
What hearts or lives have you detained
    By senseless miracle?
Above, around thy seeming sway
There bends one mighty destiny,
In whom all joys and woes contained,
    A glorious promise tell.

TO A SEA GULL.

Wild thing of loveliness wanton and free,
Fair creature that revels above the fierce sea,
Bird of the atmosphere winging and swaying
Where storm clouds are bursting and wild tempests
    playing,

To A Sea Gull.

How lightsome and airily floating and flowing
You sport where the breakers their white spray are
    throwing,
How buoyant you rest on the slow heaving tide,
Like a lover asleep in the lap of his bride.

Oh sea gull, frail beautiful bird of the wave,
With plumage so snowy and spirit so brave,
Some soul freed from earth in your frail form is
    dwelling,
Some angel of God your far course is compelling.

SONNET ON THE TIMES.

Alas, the dreary world is ill at ease,
With restless chafing straining through the day,
Amazedly beholding vast array
Of riches clutched by avarice to please
Its glutton greed with feast of miseries,
Hoarding the dreary gains while sad hearts pray
Some simple boon their anguish to allay,
To mitigate their dreaded destinies.
Oh restless age of poverty and gold,
Fate sternly ponders thy dissentient mood;
Amid the thickened clouds that darkly fold
Thy gloomy features, lurks the bitter brood
Of want and anarchy, with spirits bold
To flout thee in thy sullen solitude.

IN A LONELY MOUNTAIN GLEN.
(From a painting by William Keith)

A FOREST LONGING.

Far from busy haunts of men,
In a lonely mountain glen,
    Where the throbbing
    And the sobbing
Million hearts are faintly heard,
    Dimly wailing in the sighing
    Of the pine-tree, or the dying
Echo of some forest bird,

I am seeking, day by day,
Some stray flower on my way;
    And I ponder
    As I wander,
Ponder on the world afar,
    On the universe of sorrow
    Breaking forth on each new morrow,
Weeping like a falling star.

It is cold amid the pines,
And the sun but faintly shines
    Through the raining
    And complaining
Of the winter wind that moans;
    And the flower I seek is shrinking
    In the loam, while I am thinking
Of the troubled world that groans.

Oh could I but find that flower!
Oh had I the magic power,
    By some spelling,
    Of compelling
It to grow where all might see!
    I would nurse its tender passion,
    Nourish it in such a fashion
It would live eternally.

FREEDOM TRIUMPHANT.

Hail, child of Freedom! hail ecstatic star
   That blazed upon the wide world's darkening
      west!
Herculean nursling—fate descried afar
   What glorious promise did your birth invest;
What thraldoms shaken to the wild winds free
Would rend the ebon mask of liberty;
What throes of bloody passion, thrilling pain,
Convulsing agony would brave to gain
Immortal life, the blesséd destiny
Serene and calm amid eternity.

Hail, loved republic! realm foredoomed to stand
   Supreme amid the wavering sway of fate,
Beholding kingdoms totter from the land,
   And shrines once cherished, cold and desolate:
Thou knowest thy burning mission; thou hast
      heard
Direct from God the consecrated word
Sounding amid the hurried years that sweep

Thy impulse onward, upward, steep on steep,
Surcharging thy onspeeding hopes that gird
The very skies thou wing'st like soaring bird.

Hail, loved America! fond name that peals
    Like seraph trumpet's blast to patriot ear,
Inciting thoughts so deep the heart conceals
    This inmost meaning, lest the image dear
Too brightly should inflame the fervent breast,
And vex the thrilling soul with thoughts too blest.
Like ocean's anthem hurled about the sphere
Thy voice continuous sounds from year to year,
While mightier tasks through ripening years attest
The realm attuned to heaven's sublime behest.

Oh sacred nation, should the sordid stain
    Of bonds enslaving taint again thy state,
Should men in thy confines be crushed again,—
    Should Mammon, knocking at thy temple gate,
Gain entrance, quelling stifled hearts that cry,
Oppressed and weak, for banished liberty—
Oh, let me then escape thy cursed land

Debased and fallen! Let me rather stand
An alien in an alien realm to die,
Lamenting thy despised inconstancy.

No, no, base slanderer of my country's fame,
   Dare not oppose fate's purposed will sublime,
Predict not tyrant rule nor despot shame
   The bitter fruit of constant toiling time.
No slavish minions, bred by grasping lust,
Shall tread thy heroes' fame to filthy dust,
No tyrant lordlings mocking honor's right
Shall ever wrest the sway of freedom's might;
Now and forever shall thy sacred trust
In heavenward pantings prove thy purpose just.

OH BLESSED HOPE STILL DREAM.

Oh blessed hope still dream,
    Still live and dream and see
The fitful flames that shoot and stream
    Across the darkness free,
    Startling the world to thoughts of liberty.

Oh blessed love, still dwell
    In weary hearts that pine,
With whispered voice and tender spell
    Still show the world that thine—
    Thine is the only tone that speaks divine.

Oh blessed trust of man,
    Let no black-clad despair,
Haunting the world with visage wan,
    From some fell midnight lair
    Spring at your throat and root his tushes there.

Oh Blessed Hope Still Dream.

We live in God's own world,
   His heart is ever here;
In every bud His thought is furled,
   His presence ever near
   Reveals itself in every passion dear.

We share this realm divine
   With the eternal King;
Our hopes, like tendrils of the vine,
   To His must ever cling—
   Scorning support from any lesser thing.

We, too, His realm create,
   Each soul a vital power,
Startling itself with thoughts elate,
   Advances hour by hour,
   Winning its part of God's immortal dower.

Oh hope, oh love, oh soul,
   Oh universe of joy,
Why seems thy distant cherished goal
   So hedged with fierce annoy,
   Environed so to tempt us and destroy?

THE ETERNAL SECRET.

Oh world-sphinx vast, remote, austere,
Delving amid the inmost place
Where death and darkness seek embrace
In their wild unfooted haunt severe,
Where the progeny of th' howling gale
Chafe in their cave without avail,
Moaning for liberty—to try their wings
Where the siren sings,
And the storm fiend swings
O'er the sheeted sea
Perpetually.
Oh world-sphinx, how serene and far,
And how immutable you seem to me,
With steadfast gaze upon each star
That throbs and throbs so silently.
Thou art not like thy Memphian sister, stone,
Hewn by the antique dwellers of the Nile,
Thou art without a peer, aloof, alone,
Resting upon eternity's dark pile.
I cannot see thee tho' I know thy resting place,

What mortal ever gazed upon thy awful face?
Somewhere amid the solitude of night,
Or where the forest breathed in still delight,
Or on the sea when tempests mocked the day—
Listening in tranced delight of sweet dismay
Somewhere I heard thy voice—I heard thee say,
"Forever!"
Oh never,
Never can I imbued with that one sound
Resist the heart's elate, exulting bound
At thought of that "Forever!"
Oh thou art builded not of flesh or stone,
Thou canst not die, thou hast not grown,
Oh thou eternal secret of the spheres,
Thou spirit casting from thy thought the years
That bear the world resistless on their tide,
Thou sphinx thou art a man! I open wide
My eyes and see thy form at last, at last.
Thou art all thought, all music, all delight,
All pain, all sorrow, all the dreams of night,
Thou art my brother—how the thoughts teem fast,

Thou art myself and now I start aghast
To see the world so mirrored forth in me,
To know that I am of eternity,
To know that all is soul and soul is free,
To know that life can conquer misery!

FAREWELL TO THE MOUNTAINS.

Dream of beauty, land of splendor,
    Shrine of Nature's inmost heart,
Teeming joy thy haunts engender,
    Heaven's delight thy scenes impart.

Mountain wilderness secluded,
    Hedged with clustering groves of pine,
Haunt of Nature unobtruded,
    Crowned with buds and wreathèd vines,

Farewell to the Mountains.

Crystal fountains down thy swelling
    Slopes are leaping toward the sea,
While thy silent scenes are telling
    Tales of boundless love to me.

Must I leave thy haunts endearing,
    Paths that lead to fern-paved bowers,
Haunts where timid deer are peering
    Through a screen of wanton flowers?

Thy fond scenes are trebly cherished
    For the passion there inlaid,
For the frantic love that nourished
    Longings thirsting for its aid.

Then farewell my mountain dwelling,
    Love's sequestered bowery vale,
Time's impatient stride compelling,
    Bears me far from thy loved dale.

A Light Through the Storm.

Now to mingle 'mid the busy
    Hum of restless city's din,
Roaring 'till the mind grows dizzy,
    Reeling with its woe and sin.

There to live and there to squander
    Life's unrestful span in care,
There in aimless search to wander,
    Finding nothing good and fair.

No, no, no, a higher meaning
    Throbs amid the city's life,
And a deeper truth is screening
    Dark its form in sin and strife.

With the torch of love bright glowing
    I will seek the secret spring,
Bubbling through the filth, and showing
    Light and good in everything.

TO A THRUSH.

Oh calm and restful gloaming,
   With dubious light,
When beetles start to roaming
   And moths to flight;
When from the west is dying
   The roseate hue,
And length'ning shades are lying
   In mystic blue,
I love your silent dreaming,
   And yon lone star,
Jove's lamp, or sudden streaming
   Of meteor far.

I love to hear the quavering
   High trembling tone

Of hidden insect wavering
    'Twixt grass and stone;
And then when, breathless, waiting,
    The air is still,
A voice, full, undulating,
    With many a thrill,
Is launched, melodious, tender,
    From yonder dell—
Such thoughts it does engender
    As wizard spell.

Oh voice, oh thrush, oh fairy,
    Whate'er you be
So full, so light and airy,
    So rich and free;
I love you far more dearly
    Than all the rest
Of evening's joys; more nearly
    Your panting breast
Speaks of my own wild longing—
    Those hopes and fears
Impetuously thronging
    Upon the years.

IN SOME FAR FASTNESS OF THY WIDE DEMESNE.
(From a painting by William Keith)

REFLECTIONS ON FINDING THE SKELETON OF A DEER IN THE FOREST.

Offspring of freedom and the mountain airs,
Supreme amid thy undiscovered lairs
Where pluméd ferns droop tenderly and green,
In some far fastness of thy wide demesne
Where fretted tracery of the tangled trees
Enlaces o'er thy head, as if to please
Thy timid fancy with a gloaming light
At noonday, or to shield thy sudden flight,
I love to see
The wild exuberant glee
Of thy light leaping so tumultuously.

Oh large-eyed creature, delicately made,
The sportive wind in garb of flesh arrayed,
Thou monarch of the mountains, antler-crowned,
Thou leaping thought, transcending at a bound

Eternal laws of nature; like the arrow
Ignoring earth and everything too narrow
For perfect freedom—till, alas the day,
Thy fate o'ermasters thee, and petty clay
Becomes once more
As humble as before,
And now we spurn what erst we did adore.

I fain would think thee higher than the clod
Whereon with careless step I recent trod—
Wild wanderer of the forest! At thy birth
A soul looked out upon the gladsome earth
And gloried in the power, the joy, the light
Of simple living,—in the sunshine bright,
The tender buds and browse, the summer air,
In all things to the senses good and fair.
I grieve to find
Such tokens of a mind,
Now tenantless and vacant here enshrined.

The scrutiny of science might proclaim
Strange store of meaning in this ruined frame,

Reflections.

Behold in every bone the mark sublime
Of adaptations wrought by ceaseless time,
Interpreting as God's last miracle
Each modulation shaped so deftly well.
Thus let them read the word divine revealed
In each concrete expression.   But concealed
I see behind
These bones a vanished mind,—
The token of a soul now unconfined.

NATURE'S HARMONIES.

Oh mighty harmonies of ever-changing mood,
Reverberating through the awful solitude,
Where nature's heavenly choir exalts in loud
    proclaim
The ever-living God, that peoples her domain
With untold love and beauty—sounds that ever sing
In tender breathing pines or frantic hurrying
Of wintry tempests, does some constant aim attend
Your voicing, to embody the eternal end

Of all creation in articulate tones that tell,
Each one some fragment of the love we know so
 well?
You, merry meadow-lark that bubbles from the
 grain
Your tinkling threnody of liquid song, what strain
Of human art could pour diviner breath upon
The morning's misty verdure ere the sun has shone?
And you, sweet-scented pines that wage incessant
 sighs
And multitudinous murmurings till the whispering
 dies
In half-felt spirit breaths that slumber and yet dream
Of airy clouds fantastic through the blue that stream,
Tell me what prayer divine inspires such fainting
 tones
Of subtle beauty throbbing through ætherial zones?
But thou, oh surging ocean, awfullest, most sublime
Of pow'rs that lash against the frantic rush of time,
Fierce in thy grandeur, wild, perpetual in thy roar,
With foamy sullen boomings hurling to the shore

Thy sheltering mountains, loud is thy vast thunder-
    ing strain
Of might, immensity, and all that in the name
Of the Creator stands for power above the check
Of earthly limits paling at his certain beck.
O God, amidst thy wondrous sounds, perplexed,
    I pause,
Uncertain which seems best, or which my heart
    most awes,
Until the tone of one fair soul, attuned to all
Of Nature's beauty, echoing sweet her faintest call,
Chimes on my raptured sense, and then indeed I
    know
The tenderest breathings thou hast ever breathed
    to show,
O God, the depths of thy rich love for ardent
    hearts that glow.

VOICES THAT SPEAK IN MOURNFUL MELODY.

Voices that speak in mournful melody
Their plaintive murmur ere they die,
Souls that have burst their mortal sphere,
In tender love still lingering near,
A heavenly phantasy—
I hear! I hear!
Faces infused with holy joy,
Beaming serene of dread annoy,
Like milk white rose impearled with dew,
Transfixed eternal where it grew,
Lovely perpetually,
I see! I see!
Oh might I hold one melting tone
Forever near my soul, my very own,
Oh might one glance through all eternity
Be still transfixed unto my own, to be
My life, my love, my hope, my destiny,
Oh joy, oh love of vast serenity!
My heart beats mad to think that this might be.

FOOTPRINTS BY THE SEA.

By the solemn sounding ocean
With its mystery of motion,
With its cadences of sounding,
With its beating and its pounding,
With its melody unending,
With its elements contending,
By the sea with ceaseless beating,
I was walking and repeating
Fragments of its rhythmic voicing,
Snatches of its vast rejoicing,
When I spied a footprint trending
Down the mighty shore unending,
And I followed where it took me,
Followed, though my hope forsook me,
Followed down the sandy beaches,
Each that idly onward reaches.
Still I walk beside the ocean
And a weird untold emotion
Thrills me when I hear its beating,
When I hear my heart repeating
Beat for beat its mighty pounding
With its mystery of sounding.

THE UNKNOWN REGION.

"*Darest thou now, O soul,*
Walk out with me toward the unknown region,
Where neither ground is for the feet nor any path to follow?"
—WALT WHITMAN.

Hand and hand with the angel of Death, when the breast has ceased heaving,
When the joys and the pains of the world, and dear friends you are leaving,
Oh, my soul, dare you walk through the shadow that leads toward the light,
Dare you venture across the dark moor in the thick of the night?
Where trendest thou, soul, through the ages, what end do you see,
Are you seeking for rest and content, do you long to be free,

Are you striving for betterment endless, for growth without bound,
For love that transcends earthly longings, that round after round
Reaches upward and upward forever with limitless pain,
With the sorrow of ages to crush it and heaven to gain?
To the goodness that baffles your strivings and leaves you in tears,
To feel how sublime is the meaning that swells thro' the years,
The meaning that ever eludes you, and sweeps on its way
As dauntless you struggle to reach it, as day after day
You walk through that region of darkness, through that region unknown,
'Till the light of the future beams on you, for your woe to atone.

www.ingramcontent.com/pod-product-compliance
Lightning Source LLC
Chambersburg PA
CBHW031500160426
43195CB00010BB/1045